Revd: George Herbert ; died 24 th. February 1633

CRANE CLASSICS

GEORGE HERBERT
SELECTED POEMS

CRANE CLASSICS

George Herbert

Selected Poems

Selected and introduced by
Anthony Eyre

MOUNT ORLEANS
PRESS

Crane Classics Poetry Series
Series editor: Anthony Eyre

This collection first published in 2020 by
Mount Orleans Press
23 High Street, Cricklade SN6 6AP
https://anthonyeyre.com

CIP data for this title are available from the British Library

Typography and book production by Anthony Eyre

ISBN 978-1-912945-17-7

Printed in the UK
by the Short Run Press Ltd
Exeter

Frontispiece:
George Herbert, print after the
portrait by Robert White

CONTENTS

GEORGE HERBERT stands with Gerard Manley Hopkins in the intensity of his religious beliefs and the emotion with which he was able to express them. As a young man he wrote to his mother that his writing "shall all be, and ever consecrated to God's glory". The conflicts within Herbert, the suppression of worldly ambition in favour of a passionate devotion, provide the pulse and life-blood of his poetry. Samuel Taylor Coleridge argued that to understand Herbert we also must have an experience of this all consuming love: "Herbert is a true poet, but a poet *sui generis*, the merits of whose poems will never be felt without a sympathy with the mind and character of the man. It is not enough that the reader possess a cultivated judgment and a classical taste, unless he be likewise a Christian, a zealous and orthodox, a devout and devotional Christian. But even this will not suffice. He must be an affectionate and dutiful son of the Church." Where Coleridge was probably wrong was in maintaining the reader had to have a further affection and loyalty to the Anglican high church; Herbert's appeal is more universal and his influence is marked in poets outside that tradition.

Herbert was born in 1593, one of ten children to Richard Herbert and Magdalen, née Newport. On both sides of his family he had a distinguished background, the Herberts being Lords of Cherbury and related to the Earls of Pembroke, and the Newports being a titled and landed family from Shropshire. Richard Herbert died when George was just three and a half, and subsequently his widow Magdalen moved the family to London, where she remarried to Sir John Danvers (later one of the signatories of Charles I's death warrant). In 1629 George Herbert married his step-father's cousin Jane Danvers.

Herbert's mother Magdalen was an important inluence; an intelligent and religious woman, she was a close friend of John Donne, who spoke at her funeral in 1627. She sent George to Westminster School, from where he went on to Trinity College, Cambridge. Here he shone and dazzled in the pastures of academe, being appointed in 1620 to the position of Public Orator for the University of Cambridge. This brought him into Court circles, where the favour of James I and the friendship of Francis Bacon might have made him hope for a glittering career in public life. This certainly is the traditional view as proposed by Izaak Walton in his *Life of Mr George Herbert* (1670). James I died in 1625, and Bacon lost his place at Court; it was at this point that Herbert turned to the Church, having been ordained a deacon at the end of 1624.

These two sides of his career, the wordly and the humble, form a strong theme through his work. His vocation was a powerful one, making his poems a joy to read.

Music was another passion: he played, and obviously enjoyed playing, the lute. Like Bach, he clearly felt that music revealed God in ways beyond our powers of description—mystical, magical and mathematical:

> *My musick shall finde thee, and every string*
> *Shall have his attribute to sing;*
> *That all together may accord in thee,*
> *And prove one God, one harmonie.*

The only poems Herbert published in his lifetine were his Latin ones written in an official capacity at Cambridge and Court. Shortly before he died in 1633 he sent his manuscripts to his friend Nicholas Ferrar at the christian community he had set up in Little Gidding. Ferrar published them the same year in the collection *The Temple*.

THE ALTAR

A broken A L T A R , Lord, thy servant rears,
Made of a heart and cemented with tears:
  Whose parts are as thy hand did frame;
  No workman's tool hath touch'd the same.
          Λ H E A R T alone
          Is such a stone,
          As nothing but
          Thy pow'r doth cut.
          Wherefore each part
          Of my hard heart
          Meets in this frame,
          To praise thy name:
  That if I chance to hold my peace,
  These stones to praise thee may not cease.
Oh, let thy blessed S A C R I F I C E be mine,
And sanctify this A L T A R to be thine.

THE SACRIFICE

OH ALL YE, who passe by, whose eyes and minde
To worldly things are sharp, but to me blinde;
To me, who took eyes that I might you finde:
                              Was ever grief like mine?

The Princes of my people make a head
Against their Maker: they do wish me dead,
Who cannot wish, except I give them bread;
                              Was ever grief like mine?

Without me each one, who doth now me brave,
Had to this day been an Egyptian slave.
They use that power against me, which I gave:
                              Was ever grief like mine?

Mine own Apostle, who the bag did beare,
Though he had all I had, did not forbeare
To sell me also, and to put me there:
                              Was ever grief like mine?

For thirtie pence he did my death devise,
Who at three hundred did the ointment prize,
Not half so sweet as my sweet sacrifice:
                              Was ever grief like mine?

Therefore my soul melts, and my hearts deare treasure
Drops bloud (the onely beads) my words to measure:
O let this cup passe, if it be thy pleasure:
                              Was ever grief like mine?

GEORGE HERBERT

These drops being temper'd with sinners tears
A Balsome are for both the Hemispheres:
Curing all wounds, but mine; all, but my fears:
                    Was ever grief like mine?

Yet my Disciples sleep; I cannot gain
One houre of watching; but their drowsie brain
Comforts not me, and doth my doctrine stain:
                    Was ever grief like mine?

Arise, arise, they come. Look how they runne!
Alas! what haste they make to be undone!
How with their lanterns do they seek the sunne!
                    Was ever grief like mine?

With clubs and staves they seek me, as a thief,
Who am the way & Truth, the true relief;
Most true to those, who are my greatest grief:
                    Was ever grief like mine?

Judas, dost thou betray me with a kisse?
Canst thou finde hell about my lips? and misse
Of life, just at the gates of life and blisse?
                    Was ever grief like mine?

See, they lay hold on me, not with the hands
Of faith, but furie: yet at their commands
I suffer binding, who have loos'd their bands
                    Was ever grief like mine?

All my Disciples flie; fear puts a barre
Betwixt my friends and me. They leave the starre,
That brought the wise men of the East from farre.
                    Was ever grief like mine?

Then from one ruler to another bound
They leade me; urging, that it was not sound
What I taught: Comments would the test confound.
                              Was ever grief like mine?

The Priest and rulers all false witnesse seek
'Gainst him, who seeks not life, but is the meek
And readie Paschal Lambe of this great week:
                              Was ever grief like mine?

Then they accuse me of great blasphemie,
That I did thrust into the Deitie,
Who never thought that any robberie:
                              Was ever grief like mine?

Some said, that I the Temple to the floore
In three dayes raz'd, and raised as before.
Why, he that built the world can do much more:
                              Was ever grief like mine?

Then they condemne me all with that same breath,
Which I do give them daily, unto death.
Thus *Adam* my first breathing rendereth:
                              Was ever grief like mine?

They binde, and leade me unto *Herod*: he
Sends me to *Pilate*. This makes them agree;
But yet their friendship is my enmitie:
                              Was ever grief like mine?

Herod and all his bands do set me light,
Who teach all hands to warre, fingers to fight,
And onely am the Lord of Hosts and might:
                              Was ever grief like mine?

GEORGE HERBERT

Herod in judgement sits, while I do stand;
Examines me with a censorious hand:
I him obey, who all things else command:
                    Was ever grief like mine?

The *Jews* accuse me with dispitefulnesse;
And vying malice with my gentlenesse,
Pick quarrels with their onely happinesse:
                    Was ever grief like mine?

I answer nothing, but with patience prove
If stonie hearts will melt with gentle love.
But who does hawk at eagles with a dove?
                    Was ever grief like mine?

My silence rather doth augment their crie;
My dove doth back into my bosome flie,
Because the raging waters still are high:
                    Was ever grief like mine?

Heark how they crie aloud still, *Crucifie*:
It is not fit he live a day, they crie,
Who cannot live lesse then eternally:
                    Was ever grief like mine?

Pilate, a stranger, holdeth off; but they,
Mine owne deare people, cry, *Away, away*,
With noises confused frighting the day:
                    Was ever grief like mine?

Yet still they shout, and crie, and stop their eares,
Putting my life among their sinnes and fears,
And therefore wish *my bloud on them and theirs*:
                    Was ever grief like mine?

See how spite cankers things. These words aright
Used, and wished, are the whole worlds light:
But hony is their gall, brightnesse their night:
                      Was ever grief like mine?

They choose a murderer, and all agree
In him to do themselves a courtesie:
For it was their own case who killed me:
                      Was ever grief like mine?

And a seditious murderer he was:
But I the Prince of peace; peace that doth passe
All understanding, more then heav'n doth glasse:
                      Was ever grief like mine?

Why, Caesar is their onely King, not I:
He clave the stonie rock, when they were drie;
But surely not their hearts, as I well trie:
                      Was ever grief like mine?

Ah! how they scourge me! yet my tendernesse
Doubles each lash: and yet their bitternesse
Windes up my grief to a mysteriousnesse:
                      Was ever grief like mine?

They buffet him, and box him as they list,
Who grasps the earth and heaven with his fist,
And never yet, whom he would punish, miss'd:
                      Was ever grief like mine?

Behold, they spit on me in scornfull wise,
Who by my spittle gave the blinde man eies,
Leaving his blindnesse to my enemies:
                      Was ever grief like mine?

                                    GEORGE HERBERT

My face they cover, though it be divine.
As *Moses* face was vailed, so is mine,
Lest on their double-dark souls either shine:
                      Was ever grief like mine?

Servants and abjects flout me; they are wittie:
Now prophesie who strikes thee, is their dittie.
So they in me denie themselves all pitie:
                      Was ever grief like mine?

And now I am deliver'd unto death,
Which each one calls for so with utmost breath,
That he before me well nigh suffereth:
                      Was ever grief like mine?

Weep not, deare friends, since I for both have wept
When all my tears were bloud, the while you slept:
Your tears for your own fortunes should be kept:
                      Was ever grief like mine?

The souldiers lead me to the common hall;
There they deride me, they abuse me all:
Yet for twelve heav'nly legions I could call:
                      Was ever grief like mine?

Then with a scarlet robe they me aray;
Which shews my bloud to be the onely way
And cordiall left to repair mans decay:
                      Was ever grief like mine?

Then on my head a crown of thorns I wear:
For these are all the grapes *Sion* doth bear,
Though I my vine planted and watred there:
                      Was ever grief like mine?

So sits the earths great curse in *Adams* fall
Upon my head: so I remove it all
From th' earth unto my brows, and bear the thrall:
                                  Was ever grief like mine?

Then with the reed they gave to me before,
They strike my head, the rock from thence all store
Of heav'nly blessings issue evermore:
                                  Was ever grief like mine?

They bow their knees to me, and cry, *Hail king*:
What ever scoffes & scornfulnesse can bring,
I am the floore, the sink, where they it fling:
                                  Was ever grief like mine?

Yet since mans scepters are as frail as reeds,
And thorny all their crowns, bloudie their weeds;
I, who am Truth, turn into truth their deeds:
                                  Was ever grief like mine?

The souldiers also spit upon that face,
Which Angels did desire to have the grace,
And Prophets, once to see, but found no place:
                                  Was ever grief like mine?

Thus trimmed, forth they bring me to the rout,
Who *Crucifie him*, crie with one strong shout.
God holds his peace at man, and man cries out:
                                  Was ever grief like mine?

They leade me in once more, and putting then
Mine own clothes on, they leade me out agen.
Whom devils flie, thus is he toss'd of men:
                                  Was ever grief like mine?

GEORGE HERBERT

And now wearie of sport, glad to ingrosse
All spite in one, counting my life their losse,
They carrie me to my most bitter crosse:
                    Was ever grief like mine?

O all ye who passe by, behold and see;
Man stole the fruit, but I must climbe the tree;
The tree of life to all, but onely me:
                    Was ever grief like mine?

Lo, here I hang, charg'd with a world of sinne,
The greater world o' th' two; for that came in
By words, but this by sorrow I must win:
                    Was ever grief like mine?

Such sorrow as, if sinfull man could feel,
Or feel his part, he would not cease to kneel.
Till all were melted, though he were all steel:
                    Was ever grief like mine?

But, *O my God, my God!* why leav'st thou me,
The sonne, in whom thou dost delight to be?
My God, my God—
                    Never was grief like mine.

Shame tears my soul, my bodie many a wound;
Sharp nails pierce this, but sharper that confound;
Reproches, which are free, while I am bound.
                    Was ever grief like mine?

Now heal thy self, Physician; now come down.
Alas! I did so, when I left my crown
And fathers smile for you, to feel his frown:
                    Was ever grief like mine?

In healing not my self, there doth consist
All that salvation, which ye now resist;
Your safetie in my sicknesse doth subsist:
                              Was ever grief like mine?

Betwixt two theeves I spend my utmost breath,
As he that for some robberie suffereth.
Alas! what have I stollen from you? Death.
                              Was ever grief like mine?

A king my title is, prefixt on high;
Yet by my subjects am condemn'd to die
A servile death in servile companie:
                              Was ever grief like mine?

They give me vineger mingled with gall,
But more with malice: yet, when they did call,
With Manna, Angels food, I fed them all:
                              Was ever grief like mine?

They part my garments, and by lot dispose
My coat, the type of love, which once cur'd those
Who sought for help, never malicious foes:
                              Was ever grief like mine?

Nay, after death their spite shall further go;
For they will pierce my side, I full well know;
That as sinne came, so Sacraments might flow:
                              Was ever grief like mine?

But now I die; now all is finished.
My wo, mans weal: and now I bow my head.
Onely let others say, when I am dead,
                              Never was grief like mine.

THE THANKSGIVING

Oh King of grief! (a title strange, yet true,
> To thee of all kings onely due)
Oh King of wounds! how shall I grieve for thee,
> Who in all grief preventest me?
Shall I weep bloud? why, thou hast wept such store
> That all thy body was one doore.
Shall I be scourged, floutted, boxed, sold?
> 'Tis but to tell the tale is told.
My God, my God, why dost thou part from me?
> Was such a grief as cannot be.
Shall I then sing, skipping thy dolefull storie,
> And side with thy triumphant glorie?
Shall thy stokes be my stroking? thorns, my flower?
> Thy rod, my posie? crosse, my bower?
But how then shall I imitate thee, and
> Copie thy fair, though bloudie hand?
Surely I will revenge me on thy love,
> And trie who shall victorious prove.
If thou dost give me wealth, I will restore
> All back unto thee by the poore.
If thou dost give me honour, men shall see,
> The honour doth belong to thee.
I will not marry; or, if she be mine,
> She and her children shall be thine.
My bosome friend, if he blaspheme thy name,
> I will tear thence his love and fame.
One half of me being gone, the rest I give
> Unto some Chappell, die or live.
As for thy passion—But of that anon,
> When with the other I have done.

For thy predestination I'le contrive,
      That three yeares hence, if I survive,
I'le build a spittle, or mend common wayes,
      And mend mine own without delayes.
Then I will use the works of thy creation,
      As if I us'd them but for fashion.
The world and I will quarrell; and the yeare
      Shall not perceive, that I am here.
My musick shall finde thee, and ev'ry string
      Shall have his attribute to sing;
That all together may accord in thee,
      And prove one God, one harmonie.
If thou shalt give me wit, it shall appeare,
      If thou hast give'n it me, 'tis here.
Nay, I will reade thy book, and never move
      Till I have found therein thy love,
Thy art of love, which I'le turn back on thee:
      O my deare Saviour, Victorie!
Then for thy passion—I will do for that—
      Alas, my God, I know not what.

THE AGONIE

PHILOSOPHERS have measur'd mountains,
    Fathom'd the depths of seas, of states, and kings,
Walk'd with a staffe to heav'n, and traced fountains:
    But there are two vast, spacious things,
The which to measure it doth more behove:
Yet few there are that sound them; Sinne and Love.

    Who would know Sinne, let him repair
Unto mount Olivet; there shall he see
A man so wrung with pains, that all his hair,
    His skinne, his garments bloudie be.
Sinne is that presse and vice, which forceth pain
To hunt his cruell food through ev'ry vein.

    Who knows not Love, let him assay
And taste that juice, which on the crosse a pike
Did set again abroach; then let him say
    If ever he did taste the like.
Love in that liquour sweet and most divine,
Which my God feels as bloud; but I, as wine.

REDEMPTION

HAVING been tenant long to a rich Lord,
      Not thriving, I resolved to be bold,
      And make a suit unto him, to afford
A new small-rented lease, and cancell th' old.

In heaven at his manour I him sought:
      They told me there, that he was lately gone
      About some land, which he had dearly bought
Long since on earth, to take possession.

I straight return'd, and knowing his great birth,
      Sought him accordingly in great resorts;
      In cities, theatres, gardens, parks, and courts:
At length I heard a ragged noise and mirth

      Of theeves and murderers: there I him espied,
      Who straight, *Your suit is granted*, said, & died.

EASTER

RISE HEART; thy Lord is risen. Sing his praise
                       Without delayes,
Who takes thee by the hand, that thou likewise
                       With him mayst rise:
That, as his death calcined thee to dust,
His life may make thee gold, and much more, just.

Awake, my lute, and struggle for thy part
                       With all thy art.
The crosse taught all wood to resound his name,
                       Who bore the same.
His stretched sinews taught all strings, what key
Is best to celebrate this most high day.

Consort both heart and lute, and twist a song
                       Pleasant and long:
Or, since all musick is but three parts vied
                       And multiplied,
O let thy blessed Spirit bear a part,
And make up our defects with his sweet art.

       I got me flowers to straw thy way;
       I got me boughs off many a tree:
       But thou wast up by break of day,
       And brought'st thy sweets along with thee.

The Sunne arising in the East,
Though he give light, & th' East perfume;
If they should offer to contest
With thy arising, they presume.

Can there be any day but this,
Though many sunnes to shine endeavour?
We count three hundred, but we misse:
There is but one, and that one ever.

GEORGE HERBERT

EASTER-WINGS

LORD, who createdst man in wealth and store,
   Though foolishly he lost the same,
     Decaying more and more,
       Till he became
        Most poore:
        With thee
       Oh let me rise
     As larks, harmoniously,
   And sing this day thy victories:
Then shall the fall further the flight in me.

My tender age in sorrow did beginne:
   And still with sicknesses and shame
     Thou didst so punish sinne,
       That I became
        Most thinne.
        With thee
       Let me combine
     And feel this day thy victorie:
   For, if I imp my wing on thine
Affliction shall advance the flight in me.

WHEN FIRST thou didst entice to thee my heart,
                I thought the service brave:
So many joyes I writ down for my part,
                Besides what I might have
Out of my stock of naturall delights,
Augmented with thy gracious benefits.

I looked on thy furniture so fine,
                And made it fine to me:
Thy glorious houshold-stuffe did me entwine,
                And 'tice me unto thee.
Such starres I counted mine: both heav'n and earth
Payd me my wages in a world of mirth.

What pleasures could I want, whose King I served,
                Where joyes my fellows were?
Thus argu'd into hopes, my thoughts reserved
                No place for grief or fear.
Therefore my sudden soul caught at the place,
And made her youth and fiercenesse seek thy face.

At first thou gav'st me milk and sweetnesses;
                I had my wish and way:
My dayes were straw'd with flow'rs and happinesse;
                There was no moneth but May.
But with my yeares sorrow did twist and grow,
And made a partie unawares of wo.

My flesh began unto my soul in pain,
                    Sicknesses cleave my bones;
Consuming agues dwell in ev'ry vein,
                    And tune my breath to grones.
Sorrow was all my soul; I scarce beleeved,
Till grief did tell me roundly, that I lived.

When I got health, thou took'st away my life,
                    And more; for my friends die:
My mirth and edge was lost; a blunted knife
                    Was of more use then I.
Thus thinne and lean without a fence or friend,
I was blown through with ev'ry storm and winde.

Whereas my birth and spirit rather took
                    The way that takes the town;
Thou didst betray me to a lingring book,
                    And wrap me in a gown.
I was entangled in the world of strife,
Before I had the power to change my life.

Yet, for I threatned oft the siege to raise,
                    Not simpring all mine age,
Thou often didst with Academick praise
                    Melt and dissolve my rage.
I took thy sweetned pill, till I came where
I could not go away, nor persevere.

Yet lest perchance I should too happie be
                    In my unhappinesse,
Turning my purge to food, thou throwest me
                    Into more sicknesses.
Thus doth my power crosse-bias me, not making
Thine own gift good, yet me from my wayes taking.

Now I am here, what thou wilt do with me
                    None of my books will show:
I reade, and sigh, and wish I were a tree;
                    For sure then I should grow
To fruit or shade: at least some bird would trust
Her houshold to me, and I should be just.

Yet, though thou troublest me, I must be meek;
                    In weaknesse must be stout.
Well, I will change the service, and go seek
                    Some other master out.
Ah my deare God! though I am clean forgot,
Let me not love thee, if I love thee not.

GEORGE HERBERT

PRAYER (I)

PRAYER the Churches banquet, Angels age,
   Gods breath in man returning to his birth,
   The soul in paraphrase, heart in pilgrimage,
The Christian plummet sounding heav'n and earth;

Engine against th' Almightie, sinners towre,
   Reversed thunder, Christ-side-piercing spear,
   The six-daies world transposing in an houre,
A kinde of tune, which all things heare and fear;

Softnesse, and peace, and joy, and love, and blisse,
   Exalted Manna, gladnesse of the best,
   Heaven in ordinarie, man well drest,
The Milkie way, the bird of Paradise,

   Church-bels beyond the starres heard,
                    the souls bloud,
   The land of spices; something understood.

Cho.   LET ALL the world in ev'ry corner sing,
                 My God and King.

Vers.   The heav'ns are not too high,
          His praise may thither flie:
          The earth is not too low,
          His praises there may grow.

Cho.   Let all the world in ev'ry corner sing,
                 My God and King.

Vers.   The church with psalms must shout,
          No doore can keep them out:
          But above all, the heart
          Must bear the longest part.

Cho.   Let all the world in ev'ry corner sing,
                 My God and King.

THE TEMPER (1)

How should I praise thee, Lord! how should my rymes
    Gladly engrave thy love in steel,
    If what my soul doth feel sometimes,
        My soul might ever feel!

Although there were some fortie heav'ns, or more,
    Sometimes I peere above them all;
    Sometimes I hardly reach a score,
        Sometimes to hell I fall.

O rack me not to such a vast extent;
    Those distances belong to thee:
    The world's too little for thy tent,
        A grave too big for me.

Wilt thou meet arms with man, that thou dost stretch
    A crumme of dust from heav'n to hell?
    Will great God measure with a wretch?
        Shall he thy stature spell?

O let me, when thy roof my soul hath hid,
    O let me roost and nestle there:
    Then of a sinner thou art rid,
        And I of hope and fear.

Yet take thy way; for sure thy way is best:
    Stretch or contract me, thy poore debter:
    This is but tuning of my breast,
        To make the musick better.

Whether I flie with angels, fall with dust,
    Thy hands made both, and I am there:
Thy power and love, my love and trust
    Make one place ev'ry where.

GEORGE HERBERT

EMPLOYMENT (II)

HE that is weary, let him sit.
                          My soul would stirre
And trade in courtesies and wit,
                          Quitting the furre
To cold complexions needing it.

Man is no starre, but a quick coal
                          Of mortall fire;
Who blows it not, nor doth controll
                          A faint desire,
Lets his own ashes choke his soul.

When th' elements did for place contest
                          With him, whose will
Ordain'd the highest to be best;
                          The earth sat still,
And by the others is opprest.

Life is a business, not good cheer;
                          Ever in warres.
The sunne still shineth there or here,
                          Whereas the starres
Watch an advantage to appeare.

Oh that I were an Orenge-tree,
                          That busie plant!
Then should I ever laden be,
                          And never want
Some fruit for him that dressed me.

But we are still too young or old;
                    The man is gone,
Before we do our wares unfold:
                    So we freeze on,
Untill the grave increase our cold.

GEORGE HERBERT

DENIALL

WHEN my devotions could not pierce
              Thy silent eares;
Then was my heart broken, as was my verse;
           My breast was full of fears
              And disorder:

My bent thoughts, like a brittle bow,
              Did flie asunder:
Each took his way; some would to pleasures go,
           Some to the warres and thunder
              Of alarms.

As good go any where, they say,
              As to benumme
Both knees and heart, in crying night and day,
           Come, come, my God, O come,
              But no hearing.

O that thou shouldst give dust a tongue
              To crie to thee,
And then not heare it crying! all day long
           My heart was in my knee,
              But no hearing.

Therefore my soul lay out of sight,
              Untun'd, unstrung:
My feeble spirit, unable to look right,
           Like a nipt blossome, hung
              Discontented.

O cheer and tune my heartlesse breast,
                    Deferre no time;
That so thy favours granting my request,
                They and my minde may chime,
                    And mend my ryme.

VANITIE (I)

THE fleet Astronomer can bore,
And thred the spheres with his quick-piercing minde:
He views their stations, walks from doore to doore,
      Surveys, as if he had design'd
To make a purchase there: he sees their dances,
        And knoweth long before
Both their full-ey'd aspects, and secret glances.

    The nimble Diver with his side
Cuts through the working waves, that he may fetch
His dearely-earned pearl, which God did hide
      On purpose from the ventrous wretch:
That he might save his life, and also hers,
        Who with excessive pride
Her own destruction and his danger wears.

    The subtil Chymick can devest
And strip the creature naked, till he finde
The callow principles within their nest:
      There he imparts to them his minde,
Admitted to their bed-chamber, before
        They appeare trim and drest
To ordinarie suitours at the doore.

    What hath not man sought out and found,
But his deare God? who yet his glorious law
Embosomes in us, mellowing the ground
      With showres and frosts, with love & aw,
So that we need not say, Where's this command?
        Poore man, thou searchest round
To finde out *death*, but missest *life* at hand.

VERTUE

Sweet day, so cool, so calm, so bright,
The bridall of the earth and skie:
The dew shall weep thy fall to night;
                  For thou must die.

Sweet rose, whose hue angrie and brave
Bids the rash gazer wipe his eye:
Thy root is ever in its grave
                  And thou must die.

Sweet spring, full of sweet dayes and roses,
A box where sweets compacted lie;
My musick shows ye have your closes,
                  And all must die.

Onely a sweet and vertuous soul,
Like season'd timber, never gives;
But though the whole world turn to coal,
                  Then chiefly lives.

GEORGE HERBERT

THE PEARL

I KNOW the wayes of Learning; both the head
And pipes that feed the presse, and make it runne;
What reason hath from nature borrowed,
Or of it self, like a good huswife, spunne
In laws and policie; what the starres conspire,
What willing nature speaks, what forc'd by fire;
Both th' old discoveries, and the new-found seas,
The stock and surplus, cause and historie:
All these stand open, or I have the keyes:
       Yet I love thee.

I know the wayes of Honour, what maintains
The quick returns of courtesie and wit:
In vies of favours whether partie gains,
When glorie swells the heart, and moldeth it
To all expressions both of hand and eye,
Which on the world a true-love-knot may tie,
And bear the bundle, wheresoe're it goes:
How many drammes of spirit there must be
To sell my life unto my friends or foes:
       Yet I love thee.

I know the wayes of Pleasure, the sweet strains,
The lullings and the relishes of it;
The propositions of hot bloud and brains;
What mirth and musick mean; what love and wit
Have done these twentie hundred yeares, and more:
I know the projects of unbridled store:

My stuffe is flesh, not brasse; my senses live,
And grumble oft, that they have more in me
Then he that curbs them, being but one to five:
       Yet I love thee.

I know all these, and have them in my hand:
Therefore not sealed, but with open eyes
I flie to thee, and fully understand
Both the main sale, and the commodities;
And at what rate and price I have thy love;
With all the circumstances that may move:
Yet through these labyrinths, not my groveling wit,
But thy silk twist let down from heav'n to me,
Did both conduct and teach me, how by it
       To climbe to thee.

GEORGE HERBERT

MAN

My God, I heard this day,
That none doth build a stately habitation,
But he that means to dwell therein.
What house more stately hath there been,
Or can be, then is Man? to whose creation
All things are in decay.

For Man is ev'ry thing
And more: He is a tree, yet bears more fruit;
A beast, yet is, or should be more:
Reason and speech we onely bring.
Parrats may thank us, if they are not mute,
They go upon the score.

Man is all symmetrie,
Full of proportions, one limbe to another,
And all to all the world besides:
Each part may call the farthest, brother:
And head with foot hath private amitie,
And both with moons and tides.

Nothing hath got so farre,
But Man hath caught and kept it, as his prey.
His eyes dismount the highest starre:
He is in little all the sphere.
Herbs gladly cure our flesh; because that they
Finde their acquaintance there.

For us the windes do blow,
The earth doth rest, heav'n move, and fountains flow.
Nothing we see, but means our good,
As our *delight*, or as our *treasure*:
The whole is, either our cupboard of *food*,
Or cabinet of *pleasure*.

The starres have us to bed;
Night draws the curtain, which the sunne withdraws;
Musick and light attend our head.
All things unto our *flesh* are kinde
In their *descent* and *being*; to our minde
In their *ascent* and *cause*.

Each thing is full of dutie:
Waters united are our navigation;
Distinguished, our habitation;
Below, our drink; above, our meat;
Both are our cleanlinesse. Hath one such beautie?
Then how are all things neat?

More servants wait on Man,
Then he'l take notice of: in ev'ry path
He treads down that which doth befriend him,
When sicknesse makes him pale and wan.
Oh mightie love! Man is one world, and hath
Another to attend him.

Since then, my God, thou hast
So brave a Palace built; O dwell in it,
That it may dwell with thee at last!
Till then, afford us so much wit;
That, as the world serves us, we may serve thee,
And both thy servants be.

GEORGE HERBERT

LIFE

I MADE a posie, while the day ran by:
Here will I smell my remnant out, and tie
        My life within this band.
But Time did becken to the flowers, and they
By noon most cunningly did steal away,
        And wither'd in my hand.

My hand was next to them, and then my heart:
I took, without more thinking, in good part
        Times gentle admonition:
Who did so sweetly deaths sad taste convey,
Making my minde to smell my fatall day;
        Yet sugring the suspicion.

Farewell deare flowers, sweetly your time ye spent,
Fit, while ye liv'd, for smell or ornament,
        And after death for cures.
I follow straight without complaints or grief,
Since if my sent be good, I care not if
        It be as short as yours.

THE QUIP

THE MERRIE world did on a day
With his train-bands and mates agree
To meet together, where I lay,
And all in sport to geere at me.

First, Beautie crept into a rose,
Which when I pluckt not, Sir, said she,
Tell me, I pray, Whose hands are those?
But thou shalt answer, Lord, for me.

Then Money came, and chinking still,
What tune is this, poore man? said he:
I heard in Musick you had skill.
But thou shalt answer, Lord, for me.

Then came brave Glorie puffing by
In silks that whistled, who but he?
He scarce allow'd me half an eie.
But thou shalt answer, Lord, for me.

Then came quick Wit and Conversation,
And he would needs a comfort be,
And, to be short, make an Oration.
But thou shalt answer, Lord, for me.

Yet when the houre of thy designe
To answer these fine things shall come;
Speak not at large; say, I am thine:
And then they have their answer home.

GEORGE HERBERT

DIALOGUE

Sᴡᴇᴇᴛᴇꜱᴛ Sᴀᴠɪᴏᴜʀ, if my soul
    Were but worth the having,
Quickly should I then controll
    Any thought of waving.
But when all my care and pains
Cannot give the name of gains
To thy wretch so full of stains;
What delight or hope remains?

What (childe) is the ballance thine,
    Thine the poise and measure?
If I say, Thou shalt be mine;
    Finger not my treasure.
What the gains in having thee
Do amount to, onely he,
Who for man was sold, can see;
That transferr'd th'accounts to me.

But as I can see no merit,
    Leading to this favour:
So the way to fit me for it,
    Is beyond my savour.
As the reason then is thine;
So the way is none of mine:
I disclaim the whole designe:
Sinne disclaims and I resign.

That is all, if that I could
　　Get without repining;
And my clay my creature would
　　Follow my resigning.
That as I did freely part
With my glorie and desert,1
Left all joyes to feel all smart—
　　Ah! no more: thou break'st my heart.

　　　　　　　　　　　GEORGE HERBERT

HOPE

I GAVE to Hope a watch of mine: but he
                                An anchor gave to me.
Then an old prayer-book I did present:
                                And he an optick sent.
With that I gave a viall full of tears:
                                But he a few green eares.
Ah Loyterer! I'le no more, no more I'le bring:
                                I did expect a ring.

THE BUNCH OF GRAPES

Joy, I did lock thee up: but some bad man
    Hath let thee out again:
And now, me thinks, I am where I began
  Sev'n yeares ago: one vogue and vein,
  One aire of thoughts usurps my brain
I did towards Canaan draw; but now I am
Brought back to the Red sea, the sea of shame.

For as the Jews of old by Gods command
    Travell'd, and saw no town;
So now each Christian hath his journeys spann'd:
  Their storie pennes and sets us down.
  A single deed is small renown.
Gods works are wide, and let in future times;
His ancient justice overflows our crimes.

Then have we too our guardian fires and clouds;
    Our Scripture-dew drops fast:
We have our sands and serpents, tents and shrowds;
  Alas! our murmurings come not last.
  But where's the cluster? where's the taste
Of mine inheritance? Lord, if I must borrow,
Let me as well take up their joy, as sorrow.

But can he want the grape, who hath the wine?
    I have their fruit and more.
Blessed be God, who prosper'd *Noahs* vine,
  And made it bring forth grapes good store.
  But much more him I must adore,
Who of the Laws sowre juice sweet wine did make,
Ev'n God himself being pressed for my sake.

                      GEORGE HERBERT

THE PILGRIMAGE

I TRAVELL'D on, seeing the hill, where lay
　　　　　My expectation.
　　A long it was and weary way.
　　The gloomy cave of Desperation
I left on th' one, and on the other side
　　　　　The rock of Pride.

And so I came to Fancies medow strow'd
　　　　　With many a flower:
　　Fain would I here have made abode,
　　But I was quicken'd by my houre.
So to cares cops I came, and there got through
　　　　　With much ado.

That led me to the wilde of Passion, which
　　　　　Some call the wold;
　　A wasted place, but sometimes rich.
　　Here I was robb'd of all my gold,
Save one good Angell,2 which a friend had ti'd
　　　　　Close to my side.

At length I got unto the gladsome hill,
　　　　　Where lay my hope,
　　Where lay my heart; and climbing still,
　　When I had gain'd the brow and top,
A lake of brackish waters on the ground
　　　　　Was all I found.

With that abash'd and struck with many a sting
             Of swarming fears,
    I fell, and cry'd, Alas my King!
       Can both the way and end be tears?
Yet taking heart I rose, and then perceiv'd
             I was deceiv'd:

My hill was further: so I flung away,
            Yet heard a crie
    Just as I went, None goes that way
    And lives: If that be all, said I,
After so foul a journey death is fair,
            And but a chair.

THE COLLAR

I STRUCK the board, and cry'd, No more.
                              I will abroad.
          What? shall I ever sigh and pine?
My lines and life are free; free as the rode,
          Loose as the winde, as large as store.
                    Shall I be still in suit?
          Have I no harvest but a thorn
          To let me bloud, and not restore
What I have lost with cordiall fruit?
                              Sure there was wine
Before my sighs did drie it: there was corn
          Before my tears did drown it.
          Is the yeare onely lost to me?
                    Have I no bayes to crown it?
No flowers, no garlands gay? all blasted?
                    All wasted?
          Not so, my heart: but there is fruit,
                    And thou hast hands.
                    Recover all thy sigh-blown age
On double pleasures: leave thy cold dispute
Of what is fit, and not. Forsake thy cage,
                    Thy rope of sands,
Which pettie thoughts have made, and made to thee
          Good cable, to enforce and draw,
                    And be thy law,
          While thou didst wink and wouldst not see,
                    Away; take heed:
                    I will abroad.

Call in thy deaths head there: tie up thy fears.
             He that forbears
      To suit and serve his need,
             Deserves his load.
But as I rav'd and grew more fierce and wilde
             At every word,
      Me thoughts I heard one calling, *Childe!*
      And I reply'd, *My Lord.*

GEORGE HERBERT

THE PULLEY

WHEN God at first made man,
Having a glasse of blessings standing by;
Let us (said he) poure on him all we can:
Let the worlds riches, which dispersed lie,
     Contract into a span.

So strength first made a way;
Then beautie flow'd, then
wisdome, honour, pleasure:
When almost all was out, God made a stay,
Perceiving that alone of all his treasure
     Rest in the bottome lay.

For if I should (said he)
Bestow this jewell also on my creature,
He would adore my gifts in stead of me,
And rest in Nature, not the God of Nature:
     So both should losers be.

Yet let him keep the rest,
But keep them with repining restlesnesse:
Let him be rich and wearie, that at least,
If goodnesse leade him not, yet wearinesse
     May tosse him to my breast.

GRIEF

O who will give me tears? Come all ye springs,
Dwell in my head & eyes: come clouds, & rain:
My grief hath need of all the watry things,
That nature hath produc'd. Let ev'ry vein
Suck up a river to supply mine eyes,
My weary weeping eyes, too drie for me,
Unlesse they get new conduits, new supplies
To bear them out, and with my state agree.
What are two shallow foords, two little spouts
Of a lesse world? The greater is but small,
A narrow cupboard for my griefs and doubts,
Which want provision in the midst of all.
Verses, ye are too fine a thing, too wise
For my rough sorrows: cease, be dumbe and mute,
Give up your feet and running to mine eyes,
And keep your measures for some lovers lute,
Whose grief allows him musick and a ryme:
For mine excludes both measure, tune, and time.
                              Alas, my God!

GEORGE HERBERT

THE FLOWER

How fresh, O Lord, how sweet and clean
Are thy returns! ev'n as the flowers in spring;
        To which, besides their own demean,
The late-past frosts tributes of pleasure bring.
                Grief melts away
                Like snow in May,
        As if there were no such cold thing.

        Who would have thought my shrivel'd heart
Could have recover'd greennesse? It was gone
        Quite under ground; as flowers depart
To see their mother-root, when they have blown;
                Where they together
                All the hard weather,
        Dead to the world, keep house unknown.

        These are thy wonders, Lord of power,
Killing and quickning, bringing down to hell
        And up to heaven in an houre;
Making a chiming of a passing-bell,
                We say amisse,
                This or that is:
        Thy word is all, if we could spell.

        O that I once past changing were;
Fast in thy Paradise, where no flower can wither!
        Many a spring I shoot up fair,
Offring at heav'n, growing and groning thither:
                Nor doth my flower
                Want a spring-showre,
        My sinnes and I joining together;

But while I grow to a straight line;
Still upwards bent, as if heav'n were mine own,
        Thy anger comes, and I decline:
What frost to that? what pole is not the zone,
                Where all things burn,
                When thou dost turn,
        And the least frown of thine is shown?

        And now in age I bud again,
After so many deaths I live and write;
        I once more smell the dew and rain,
And relish versing: O my onely light,
                It cannot be
                That I am he
        On whom thy tempests fell all night.

        These are thy wonders, Lord of love,
To make us see we are but flowers that glide:
        Which when we once can finde and prove,
Thou hast a garden for us, where to bide.
                Who would be more,
                Swelling through store,
        Forfeit their Paradise by their pride.

BITTER-SWEET

Ah my deare angrie Lord,
Since thou dost love, yet strike;
Cast down, yet help afford;
Sure I will do the like.

I will complain, yet praise;
I will bewail, approve:
And all my sowre-sweet dayes
I will lament, and love.

THE FORERUNNERS

THE harbingers are come. See, see their mark;
White is their colour, and behold my head.
But must they have my brain? must they dispark
Those sparkling notions, which therein were bred?
      Must dulnesse turn me to a clod?
Yet have they left me, *Thou art still my God.*

Good men ye be, to leave me my best room,
Ev'n all my heart, and what is lodged there:
I passe not, I, what of the rest become,
So *Thou art still my God*, be out of fear.
      He will be pleased with that dittie;
And if I please him, I write fine and wittie.

Farewell sweet phrases, lovely metaphors.
But will ye leave me thus? when ye before
Of stews and brothels onely knew the doores,
Then did I wash you with my tears, and more,
      Brought you to Church well drest and clad:
My God must have my best, ev'n all I had.

Lovely enchanting language, sugar-cane,
Hony of roses, whither wilt thou flie?
Hath some fond lover tic'd thee to thy bane?
And wilt thou leave the Church, and love a stie?
      Fie, thou wilt soil thy broider'd coat,
And hurt thyself, and him that sings the note.

Let foolish lovers, if they will love dung,
And canvas, not with arras, clothe their shame:
Let follie speak in her own native tongue.
True beautie dwells on high: ours is a flame
            But borrow'd thence to light us thither.
Beautie and beauteous words should go together.

Yet if you go, I passe not; take your way:
For, *Thou art still my God*, is all that ye
Perhaps with more embellishment can say,
Go birds of spring: let winter have his fee,
            Let a bleak palenesse chalk the doore,
So all within be livelier then before.

DISCIPLINE

Throw away thy rod,
Throw away thy wrath:
         O my God,
Take the gentle path.

For my hearts desire
Unto thine is bent:
         I aspire
To a full consent.

Not a word or look
I affect to own,
         But by book,
And thy book alone.

Though I fail, I weep:
Though I halt in pace,
         Yet I creep
To the throne of grace.

Then let wrath remove;
Love will do the deed:
         For with love
Stonie hearts will bleed.

Love is swift of foot;
Love's a man of warre,
         And can shoot,
And can hit from farre.

                              GEORGE HERBERT

Who can scape his bow?
That which wrought on thee,
            Brought thee low,
Needs must work on me.

Throw away thy rod;
Though man frailties hath,
            Thou art God:
Throw away thy wrath.

THE ELIXIR

TEACH me, my God and King,
In all things thee to see,
And what I do in any thing,
To do it as for thee:

Not rudely, as a beast,
To runne into an action;
But still to make thee prepossest,
And give it his perfection.

A man that looks on glasse,
On it may stay his eye;
Or if he pleaseth, through it passe,
And then the heav'n espie.

All may of thee partake:
Nothing can be so mean,
Which with his tincture (for thy sake)
Will not grow bright and clean.

A servant with this clause
Makes drudgerie divine:
Who sweeps a room, as for thy laws,
Makes that and th' action fine.

This is the famous stone
That turneth all to gold:
For that which God doth touch and own
Cannot for lesse be told.

GEORGE HERBERT

LOVE (III)

LOVE bade me welcome: yet my soul drew back,
        Guiltie of dust and sinne.
But quick-ey'd Love, observing me grow slack
        From my first entrance in,
Drew nearer to me, swectly questioning,
        If I lack'd any thing.

A guest, I answer'd, worthy to be here:
        Love said, You shall be he.
I the unkinde, ungratefull? Ah my deare,
        I cannot look on thee.
Love took my hand, and smiling did reply,
        Who made the eyes but I?

Truth Lord, but I have marr'd them: let my shame
        Go where it doth deserve.
And know you not, sayes Love, who bore the blame?
        My deare, then I will serve.
You must sit down, sayes Love, and taste my meat:
        So I did sit and eat.